NO LONGER
PROPERTY OF PPLD

HAWAII

Past and Present

Joanne Mattern

rosen publishing's
rosen
central

New York

Published in 2011 by The Rosen Publishing Group, Inc.
29 East 21st Street, New York, NY 10010

Copyright © 2011 by The Rosen Publishing Group, Inc.

First Edition

All rights reserved. No part of this book may be reproduced in any form without permission in writing from the publisher, except by a reviewer.

Library of Congress Cataloging-in-Publication Data

Mattern, Joanne, 1963–
Hawaii: past and present / Joanne Mattern.—1st ed.
    p. cm. — (The United States: past and present)
Includes bibliographical references and index.
ISBN 978-1-4358-9479-2 (library binding)— ISBN 978-1-4358-9506-5 (pbk) —
ISBN 978-1-4358-9540-9 (6-pack)
1. Hawaii—Juvenile literature. I. Title.
DU623.25.M36 2011
996.9—dc22

2009050544

Manufactured in Malaysia

CPSIA Compliance Information: Batch #S10YA: For further information, contact Rosen Publishing, New York, New York, at 1-800-237-9932.

On the cover: Top left: This statue of King Kamehameha I stands in front of the Hawaii Supreme Court building in Honolulu. Top right: A tasty pineapple grows in a Hawaiian field. Bottom: The spectacular Waikiki Beach in Honolulu is one of Hawaii's top tourist attractions.

Contents

Introduction   5

Chapter 1
The Land of Hawaii   6

Chapter 2
The History of Hawaii   14

Chapter 3
The Government of Hawaii   23

Chapter 4
The Economy of Hawaii   28

Chapter 5
**People from Hawaii:
Past and Present**   32

Timeline   39

Hawaii at a Glance   40

Glossary   42

For More Information   43

For Further Reading   44

Bibliography   45

Index   47

Hawaii is the only state made up entirely of islands. It is located in the Pacific Ocean, far from the mainland.

Introduction

Hawaii is unlike any other state in the United States. Unlike the other states, Hawaii is made up of a series of volcanic islands. In addition, Hawaii is far away from the rest of the United States. It is almost 2,400 miles (3,862 kilometers) from the mainland. Hawaii is also the only state that was once ruled by its own monarchy. It was the last state to join the nation, achieving statehood in 1959.

The makeup of Hawaii's population is also different from that of other U.S. states. In reporting their ancestry, more than half the population of Hawaii identifies as Asian, Native Hawaiian, or Pacific Islander. This population mix gives the Hawaiian Islands a culture that is very different from other parts of the United States.

Hawaii is the only state that has a tropical climate across its entire area. The temperature is pleasant all year long, and the warm waters of the Pacific Ocean surround the state. Hawaii's tropical climate makes it a great place to grow a variety of fruits, including pineapples and melons, as well as other crops, such as sugar and coffee.

Hawaii has a long and complicated history, and the story of how it came to be part of the United States is very different from the stories of other states. Its government changed from a monarchy to a republic, then to a U.S. territory, and finally to a U.S. state. Hawaii holds a special place in American history and culture. Let's find out more about the tropical paradise that became America's fiftieth state.

Chapter 1

THE LAND OF HAWAII

Hawaii is the only U.S. state made up entirely of islands. Volcanoes created these islands millions of years ago. Hawaii includes 132 large and small islands that stretch more than 1,500 miles (2,414 km) in the North Pacific Ocean. This chain of islands is called the Hawaiian Archipelago.

The Islands of Hawaii

The state's islands range in size from small sandbars or coral reefs to the largest island, Hawaii, which measures 4,028 square miles (10,433 sq km) in area. Hawaii's eight largest islands are all located at the southeastern end of the archipelago. These islands contain a variety of landforms, including mountains, valleys, rain forests, and beaches.

Hawaii

Hawaii, also known as the Big Island, is the largest of the islands. It has many mountains, including Mauna Kea, which is the highest point in the state, at 13,796 feet (4,205 meters) above sea level. It is also home to another important mountain called Mauna Loa, which reaches 13,677 feet (4,169 m). These mountains have high cliffs and

Lava fills a crack in the earth at Kilauea. The current eruption at Kilauea has been taking place for more than twenty-seven years.

waterfalls, and they are tall enough that snow covers the tops of them in the winter. Below the mountains stretch miles of valleys and grasslands.

Five of the Big Island's mountains are volcanoes. Some of them are active and some are dormant, or inactive. Mauna Loa, the largest volcano on Earth, has erupted thirty-three times since 1843. Perhaps the most famous Hawaiian volcano is Kilauea. It is one of the most active volcanoes in the world. Kilauea has been erupting continuously since 1983. Its flows of lava are constantly pouring down the mountain, either on the surface or through underground tubes.

Where the lava flows into the ocean, it cools and hardens, forming new land. Kilauea's eruptions have added about 568 acres (230 hectares) of new land to Hawaii over the past twenty-seven years.

Most of Hawaii's beaches are on the northwest shore. Since the island is the youngest geologically, its beaches are smaller and rockier than those on the other islands. The southeast shore features black sand beaches formed from crushed volcanic rock.

Maui

The second largest Hawaiian island is Maui. It covers 727 square miles (1,883 sq km). Maui is shaped like an hourglass. The eastern part of the island includes Haleakala, or the East Maui Volcano, which reaches 10,023 feet (3,055 m) and has a large crater at its summit. The western part of Maui includes the smaller West Maui Volcano. An isthmus, or narrow strip of land, connects the two mountainous areas. The soil in this area is very fertile and is used to grow pineapples, sugarcane, and other crops.

Maui has more beaches than any other Hawaiian island. It's older than the Big Island, and its beaches are more sandy than rocky. The island is also known for the enormous waves that break off of its northern shore.

Kahoolawe, Lanai, and Molokai

Kahoolawe is a tiny island that lies south of Maui. Only 45 square miles (117 sq km) in land area, it is the smallest of the eight major Hawaiian Islands. Although no one lives there now, the island was once inhabited. Its grasslands were used for grazing sheep and goats. In the mid-twentieth century, the U.S. military used the island for bombing practice.

Lanai is another very small island. About three thousand people live on this island, which is 140.5 square miles (364 sq km) in area. Its highest point is Mount Lanaihale, which reaches 3,370 feet (1,027 m) on the island's eastern shore. At one time, Lanai was the center of Hawaii's pineapple industry. Today, the island is better known as a tourist attraction. Visitors enjoy Lanai's beauty, especially its clear offshore waters.

Huelo is an islet, or little island, located near the sea cliffs of Molokai. It is a state seabird sanctuary.

Molokai lies northwest of Maui and north of Lanai. This island is 260 square miles (673 sq km) and has a long, narrow shape. Its northern shore has some of the world's tallest sea cliffs. In fact, Molokai has 14 miles (22.5 km) of sea cliffs with heights of 1,000 feet (305 m) or more. The island also boasts Hawaii's tallest waterfall, Kahiwa. In contrast, the western part of Molokai is low and dry.

Oahu

Oahu has a land area of 600 square miles (1,554 sq km) and features two mountain ranges. The Koolau Range forms the eastern part of the island. The Waianae Range is on the western side of the island. A broad plateau lies between these two mountain ranges. Oahu has rain forests, waterfalls, and beautiful sandy beaches. In

Kahoolawe: From Bombs to Beauty

During World War II, no one wanted to be on the island of Kahoolawe. The U.S. Navy had been there since 1920. When the United States entered the war in 1941, the military took full control and forced the island's few inhabitants to leave Kahoolawe. From then on, the uninhabited island was used for bombing practice by American planes and was hit with torpedo strikes from American warships. The U.S. Navy and Marine Corps continued to bomb the island after the war. After decades of blasting, Kahoolawe was a lifeless wasteland full of bomb craters and debris.

The bombing practices stopped during the 1970s, and environmental groups began to study the island. In 1976, a group of Native Hawaiians formed a group called Protect Kahoolawe Ohana. This group staged many protests and sit-ins on the island, demanding that the United States turn the island over to Hawaii and let the state control it. Although several protesters were arrested and sent to prison, people in the environmental movement did not give up. In 1994, President Bill Clinton returned Kahoolawe to Hawaii's control.

Today, a lot has changed on Kahoolawe. Although there are still no residents, the island is no longer a bombed-out wasteland. Instead, it has become a place dedicated to traditional Hawaiian culture and wildlife. The Hawaii State Legislature has passed a law establishing the Kahoolawe Island Reserve. The law states that the island and its waters can only be used for Native Hawaiian cultural, spiritual, and educational purposes. Hawaii is working with environmental groups to return the island to its natural state of beauty. Unexploded munitions are being cleared from the land. The soil is being enriched and restored, and the state plans to reseed the island with native plants. The state also plans to create an educational center where people can learn about and experience traditional Hawaiian culture. Today, Kahoolawe is being transformed from a place of destruction into a place of natural and cultural beauty.

addition, its North Shore is the location of some of the best surfing in the world.

Oahu is the most heavily populated island in Hawaii. More than nine hundred thousand people, or about 70 percent of Hawaii's population, live on Oahu. The state's capital city, Honolulu, is located on the southern shore.

A surfer rides a huge wave on Oahu's North Shore during the Vans Triple Crown of Surfing competition.

Kauai and Niihau

Kauai is the northernmost of the eight main islands. It has a land area of 552 square miles (1,430 sq km). Kauai is often called the Garden Island because its soil is so fertile. The central part of the island is filled with rugged mountains and forests. Kauai also contains steep valleys, canyons, and gorges. Waimea Canyon has colorful rock walls that are almost 3,000 feet (914 m) high. For this reason, the gorge is sometimes called the Grand Canyon of the Pacific. Another notable spot is a mountain peak called Mount Waialeale, which holds the record as the wettest place in the world. The mountain receives an average of 460 inches (1,168 centimeters) of rain a year. This rain replenishes the many streams and waterfalls on the island.

Niihau is a tiny island located west of Kauai. It covers only 72 square miles (186 sq km). Fewer than three hundred people, all of Native Hawaiian ancestry, live on Niihau. These residents use the low, dry land for cattle ranching and farming. There is no tourism here, and nonresidents can only come for short visits. Although most of its land is arid, Niihau is home to Hawaii's largest lake, Halalii Lake.

Animal Life

Because Hawaii is a collection of isolated islands, the state has animal species that are found nowhere else in the world. For example, it has thousands of native insect species and twenty-three native bird species. Hawaii also has more than one thousand species of land snails with beautiful shells.

Hawaii's only native mammals are bats, seals, dolphins, and whales. However, over the centuries, many other animals were brought to the islands by settlers or stowed away aboard their ships. These animals include rats, pigs, goats, sheep, and mongooses.

In many cases, newly introduced animals have been disastrous to Hawaii. Feral pigs and goats damaged grasslands and forests by grazing there. Rats and mice ate native plants. The mongoose, which was brought to Hawaii to kill the rats, also ate the eggs of Hawaii's native birds, such as the nene (Hawaiian goose) and koloa (Hawaiian duck).

The waters around Hawaii teem with life. Hundreds of varieties of fish live in the waters near the islands. The Pacific Ocean is filled with seals, dolphins, and several species of whales, including the humpback.

Hawaii has more endangered species than any other U.S. state. More than fifty of the state's animal species are listed as endangered and threatened. Some of the endangered animals include the Hawaiian hoary bat, the Hawaiian monk seal, and the Laysan duck.

Plant Life

Most of Hawaii has a tropical climate, which makes it a paradise for trees and flowers. Hawaii has more than 1,700 flowering plants, many of which are not found anywhere else in the world. The island is home to colorful flowers such as yellow hibiscus, orchids, jasmine, frangipani, and bougainvillea. Tropical trees include the jacaranda, African tulip tree, and ohia. Hawaii also has many trees that produce tropical fruits, including bananas, coconuts, papayas, guavas, mangoes, and lychee and macadamia nuts.

Orchids, some of the most beautiful flowers in the world, are seen here growing on a farm in Oahu.

As with animals, non-native plants have threatened the native plants in Hawaii. Settlers introduced plants like clidemia, blackberries, and albesia, which have grown so well that they have pushed native plants aside. Today, almost 275 native plant species are listed as endangered or threatened.

Chapter 2

THE HISTORY OF HAWAII

People have lived on islands in the Pacific for thousands of years. Between about 300 and 600 CE, some of these islanders, the Polynesians, sailed across the South Pacific and landed on what is now Hawaii. Researchers believe these first Hawaiians may have come from islands called the Marquesas. Later, between about 800 and 1000 CE, another wave of Polynesian settlers arrived. Oral histories (stories told from generation to generation) suggest that some of these people came from the island of Tahiti.

Skilled Seafarers

Hawaii's first residents were experts at sailing and fishing. They were able to navigate the vast expanse of the Pacific Ocean just by using the stars and without using instruments like compasses to help them figure out where they were going. These new arrivals built the first villages on the islands of Hawaii and Kauai. Later, they moved onto the other islands.

Some early inhabitants settled along the coasts of the islands. These settlers became excellent fishermen. They even built fishponds to raise fish that would be easy to catch. Others lived in the mountains and valleys, where they farmed and hunted. Many of the crops they grew, such as bananas, coconuts, and taros, came from the cuttings and seeds that the early settlers had brought with them. Different groups often met to trade food and goods with each other.

Chiefs and Gods

In Native Hawaiian society, chiefs called ali'i nui ruled. The people believed the ali'i nui were descended from the gods themselves. The ali'i nui ruled with the help of priests, who were called kahunas.

Hawaiian society was divided into levels called castes. The highest caste included the ali'i nui and the next, the kahunas. The lowest class included people who were considered slaves, or outcasts. Most people belonged to a caste between the kahunas and the slaves. This caste was known as the maka'ainana (commoners) and included farmers, fishermen, and craftspeople. Everyone had to follow a strict system of social rules and laws known as the kapu system.

This portrait depicts Kamehameha I, who united the Hawaiian Islands into one kingdom in 1810.

For many years, each island had its own chief as ruler. Sometimes wars broke out between one island's people and those of another. In the 1780s, Kamehameha, the ruler of the island of Hawaii, began gathering more power. In 1795, he conquered Oahu, Maui, Lanai,

At first, Hawaii's natives welcomed Captain James Cook and his British crew. This painting shows King Terreeoboo and his men bringing gifts to the British explorer in 1779.

and Molokai. By 1810, he became Kamehameha I, the first king of all the islands.

Captain Cook and the British

This period was important for another reason. In 1778, a British explorer named Captain James Cook arrived in Hawaii on the ships *Resolution* and *Discovery*. He called the islands the Sandwich Islands, after the British Earl of Sandwich.

At first, Hawaiian natives welcomed the British. They had never seen such fair-skinned people, and they marveled at their technology and customs. The British, in turn, were surprised and pleased by how well the Hawaiians treated them.

Unfortunately, the good feelings did not last long. The Hawaiians became annoyed with the British, especially when the foreigners broke many of the native kapu. They also resented Cook's constant demands for food and supplies. Finally, in 1779, Cook went to Kealakekua Bay, Hawaii, to get one of his boats from the islanders. A fight broke out, and Cook and several of his men were murdered. The rest of his men quickly left the islands.

New Arrivals and Changes

Explorers and settlers from Europe continued to arrive in Hawaii. The islands were a good place to stop on travelers' long journeys to the Far East. Some people came to participate in trapping and whaling. By the early 1800s, small communities of Europeans began settling on the islands. These new residents came from countries such as Great Britain, France, Russia, and the United States.

As foreigners arrived, they brought new diseases with them. The native Hawaiians had no immunity to these diseases and many died. Their numbers plunged, weakening the native Hawaiian culture.

Christian missionaries also arrived in Hawaii and began to teach the natives. By 1831, more than fifty thousand Hawaiians were studying in Western-style Christian schools. In time, traditional Hawaiian beliefs began to disappear.

Another reason for the disappearance of native customs was the influence of Kamehameha I's son, Kamehameha II. When Kamehameha II became king after the death of his father in 1819, he and his queen ended the ancient kapu system that had governed Hawaiian culture.

Molokai: Lonely No More

The island of Molokai holds an important place in Hawaiian history, thanks to a much-feared disease called leprosy (now known as Hansen's disease). Leprosy first appeared in Hawaii in 1835. People were frightened of the disease, which often caused terrible disfigurement and, at the time, had no cure.

Because the disease was highly contagious, the Hawaiian government established a colony in 1865 to isolate patients. The location was Kalaupapa, a small peninsula on the northern side of Molokai. Between 1866 and 1969, more than eight thousand Hawaiians were sent to live the rest of their lives there. People were so afraid to visit Molokai that the island became known as the Lonely Island.

The Hawaiian government thought the residents of Kalaupapa would be able to farm and take care of themselves, but most of the people were too weak and sick to do so. Few people wanted to come to help them. Conditions became very unhealthy and almost inhuman. It wasn't until 1873, when a Belgian missionary known as Father Damien arrived, that conditions began to improve. Father Damien helped residents build houses and find work. He organized schools, bands, and choirs. He also gave the people spiritual guidance and hope. In 1889, Father Damien died from Hansen's disease himself.

During the twentieth century, antibiotics were discovered that could cure leprosy or keep it in check. So the need to isolate patients ended. Although the residents of Kalaupapa were allowed to leave the colony after 1969, some chose to stay. The patients had lived much of their lives there and had married and raised children.

Kalaupapa was named a National Historical Park in 1980. Visitors come to tour the remains of the old leper colony, see the tall sea cliffs that isolate the area, and learn about Father Damien's work. Kalaupapa is still a small, quiet community, but Molokai itself has become a popular tourist destination and is now called the Friendly Isle. Many people who live on the island are descended from the patients who were sent there years ago.

Businesses Take Charge

In 1835, Boston merchants sent an American named William Hooper to build the first sugar plantation in Hawaii. Just twenty years later, sugar was Hawaii's leading export and was called King Sugar. Plantations for growing sugarcane were built all over the islands. Owners hired workers from China, Japan, Korea, Puerto Rico, Europe, and the Philippines. More than three hundred thousand immigrants came to Hawaii between 1850 and 1920, forever changing the ethnic makeup of the population.

Sugarcane was not the only crop to wildly succeed in Hawaii. The islands' tropical climate was perfect for growing pineapples. In 1900, James Drummond Dole set up his first pineapple plantation in Hawaii. In 1922, Dole bought the island of Lanai and established the largest pineapple plantation in the world. Even more foreign workers and owners flocked to the islands to work in the pineapple industry.

As more wealthy business owners and landowners settled in Hawaii, they began to get involved in the islands' politics. As early as the mid-1800s, these businesspeople began to introduce democratic ideas to Hawaii. Their efforts led to some improvements, such as a written constitution, a legislature, and a supreme court. However, the reforms also meant that wealthy foreigners could pressure the monarchs and manipulate the islands' laws to benefit themselves. The powers of the monarchy began to fade.

The End of the Monarchy

By 1891, when Queen Liliuokalani came to the throne, the monarchy had very little power. The queen wanted to restore power to the monarchy, give a greater voice to Native Hawaiians, and get rid of foreign control. She opposed a treaty from 1887 that gave the United States special trade privileges, as well as the right to build a naval base at Pearl Harbor.

Liliuokalani's efforts angered American businessmen, who had many interests in the area. In 1893, a group of planters and businessmen—with the support of John Stevens, the U.S. envoy to Hawaii, and some U.S. Marines—stormed the royal palace and overthrew the queen. Soon after, a provisional (temporary) government was established in Hawaii. It was led by Sanford B. Dole, a cousin of James Dole of pineapple fame. In 1894, Dole and his supporters established the Republic of Hawaii.

At the time, President Grover Cleveland did not approve of the takeover of Hawaii. However, the U.S. Congress recognized that the islands were strategically important. In 1898, under President William McKinley, Congress voted to annex the islands. Then, in 1900, Congress made Hawaii a U.S. territory. The law granted U.S. citizenship to Hawaiians, but the islanders had no representation in the federal government. They began to work toward making Hawaii a state.

Hawaii in World War II

After the annexation of Hawaii in 1898, the U.S. Navy established a base at the port of Pearl Harbor on Oahu. On December 7, 1941, Pearl Harbor was bombed by Japanese planes. The bombing killed more than 2,400 people, mostly U.S. servicemen. For that reason, it became known as "the day that will live in infamy," in the words of President Franklin D. Roosevelt. The bombing of Pearl Harbor pushed the United States to declare war on Japan and enter World War II.

World War II was a difficult time for many Hawaiians, especially those of Japanese ancestry. Japan was now an enemy of the United States. The U.S. government and many citizens were not sure the Japanese residents of Hawaii could be trusted, even though many families had lived in Hawaii for generations. In one of the most shameful acts in U.S. history, thousands of Japanese Americans were sent to detention camps in

The naval ship USS *Shaw* explodes during the Japanese bombing of Pearl Harbor on December 7, 1941. More than 2,400 Americans lost their lives in the attack.

California, Wyoming, and other states in 1942. About 1,400 Japanese Americans from Hawaii were among them. These U.S. citizens were held as prisoners in their own country until 1944. When they finally returned to Hawaii, many found that their homes and businesses had been stolen or mismanaged by the people they left behind.

Many Japanese Americans were eager to prove their loyalty to the United States. Numerous Japanese American men from Hawaii enlisted in the U.S. Army after Pearl Harbor. For example, about 2,600 men from Hawaii and 800 men from the detention camps formed a special division called the 442nd Regimental Combat Team. It was also called the Nisei Combat Team because all of the men were sons of Japanese immigrants. The Nisei soldiers fought bravely and proved to the world that they were loyal to the United States.

The Fiftieth State

Residents of Waikiki wave newspapers and celebrate the news of Hawaii becoming the fiftieth U.S. state in 1959.

The people of Hawaii fought for statehood for many years. Progress toward this goal continued after World War II ended. In 1950, representatives met to draw up a state constitution.

Around the same time, Alaska was also trying to become a state. John A. Burns, Hawaii's representative in Congress, and the representative from Alaska, Ralph Julian Rivers, petitioned the United States for statehood at the same time. The representatives felt that Congress could not accept one state and not the other. They were right. On March 12, 1959, the Senate passed a bill admitting Hawaii to the United States. On August 21, 1959, President Dwight D. Eisenhower signed the bill into law. America now had fifty states!

In 1993, President Bill Clinton signed a bill called the Apology Resolution. The resolution apologized to the Hawaiian people for overthrowing Queen Liliuokalani one hundred years earlier, and it acknowledged that removing the monarchy had been an illegal act. Today, Hawaii is a strong and loyal state, but there are still people who would like the islands to break away and be free once more.

Chapter 3

THE GOVERNMENT OF HAWAII

In the 1800s, a monarchy governed Hawaii. In 1900, Hawaii became a U.S. territory. Since 1959, it has been one of the fifty states. Today, Hawaii's government is closely modeled after the governments of the other U.S. states, as well as the federal government. Like these other governments, Hawaii's government is divided into three branches.

The Executive Branch

The executive branch carries out state laws and runs public affairs. Hawaii's executive branch includes the governor, who is the state's chief executive, and the lieutenant governor. Hawaii's citizens elect these officials to four-year terms. If the governor cannot serve, the lieutenant governor takes his or her place. The lieutenant governor also supports the governor by heading committees and performing other duties.

Hawaii's governor has many responsibilities. One of the most important is to appoint officials to head the state's different departments, such as those for health, agriculture, and education. The governor also appoints the state's attorney general and supreme

Iolani Palace in Honolulu was once the residence of Hawaii's kings and queens. It was used as the government headquarters for the republic, territory, and state of Hawaii until 1969.

court judges. Hawaii's governor works closely with the state's legislative branch. The governor can recommend legislation. He or she can also veto, or reject, bills that the legislature passes.

The Legislative Branch

The job of the legislative branch is to make and pass laws. Hawaii's legislature has two houses. The upper house is the senate and the lower house is the house of representatives. Hawaii's senate has twenty-five state senators. Each senator represents an area called a legislative district. Senators are elected every four years. The house of representatives has fifty-one delegates. Each delegate is elected to a two-year term.

All seats are filled on opening day of the legislative session in the Hawaii State House of Representatives.

The legislature of Hawaii works to pass new laws, or bills. If a majority of the legislators vote to approve a bill, it goes to the governor to be signed into law. The governor can veto any bill, but the legislature then has the opportunity to override the veto if two-thirds of its members agree. Hawaii's legislature also approves the state budget, as well as any appointments that the governor makes.

The Judicial Branch

The judicial branch is the state's court system. Hawaii's highest court is called the supreme court. The Hawaii Supreme Court has five members, including one chief justice and four associate justices. These judges make sure that Hawaii's laws follow the state constitution.

Six judges serve on the Intermediate Court of Appeals, the next highest court in the state. These judges hear cases in panels of three.

From Tribal Society to Monarchy to Democracy

In the 1700s, chiefs and priests ruled Hawaii and enforced a traditional system of laws. Society was divided into rigid castes. A person's entire life depended on the caste into which he or she was born. A boy born into a warrior caste would grow up to be a warrior. Someone born into a slave caste had no choice but to be a slave. Only a person who was born into a family of chiefs could grow up to be a chief.

During this period, all Hawaiians followed a series of ancient rules called kapu. These rules had to be followed by everyone, from the chief ruler down to the lowliest slave. Kapu were rules for every aspect of life. One kapu stated that men and women could not eat a meal together. It was also forbidden for commoners to touch anything belonging to the chief ruler—even the ruler's shadow! Anyone who broke this kapu, even by accident, could be put to death.

When King Kamehameha I unified all the islands in 1810, Hawaii became a monarchy. His son Kamehameha II ended the kapu system in 1819, so people no longer had to follow the rules of this ancient tradition. Another son, Kamehameha III, introduced a written constitution in 1840. It established a legislature that included some elected representatives. Even with these changes, life under a monarchy was very different than life in a democracy. The monarch had enormous power, inherited the office, and ruled for life.

After Hawaii became a U.S. territory, its form of government changed greatly. After 1900, it had a governor and territorial secretary (similar to a lieutenant governor) who were appointed by the president. All citizens of Hawaii became citizens of the United States.

Today, Hawaii is governed democratically, just like every other state in the United States. The people elect government officials. Anyone can run for local or state office, no matter what kind of family he or she comes from. Also, Hawaii has an equal say in the federal government through the senators and representatives that serve in the U.S. Congress.

Below this court are many trial courts, including district courts, circuit courts, and family courts. After cases are tried in these courts, they can be appealed in the Intermediate Court of Appeals. If people don't agree with the decision of the court of appeals, they can appeal the case one last time before the supreme court of the state.

Local Government

Unlike other U.S. states, Hawaii has no city governments. Instead, the state's islands are divided into four counties: Hawaii County, Honolulu County, Kauai County, and Maui County. Each county is governed by a mayor and an elected council. Towns and cities don't have their own governments, but fall under the county's control. Even Honolulu, the capital of the state, does not have its own city government. Instead, Honolulu's city and county governments are combined.

Chapter 4

THE ECONOMY OF HAWAII

Hawaii is a tropical paradise, so it should be no surprise that tourism is its most important industry. However, tourism is not the only element that keeps Hawaii's economy strong. The state has a number of industries that employ many of its citizens.

Service and Tourism

Service is a key part of Hawaii's economy. Companies in this industry provide important services, rather than make products. Hawaii's service industry includes workers in health care, insurance, banking, education, and tourism. Real estate, computer engineering, and software development are also important parts of Hawaii's service industry.

Tourism is a major part of Hawaii's economy, bringing millions of dollars to Hawaii every year. About 20 percent of the state's income comes from tourism. Every year, visitors flock to the islands to see stunning beauty that includes beaches, volcanoes, and other natural wonders. The tourism industry employs many people in different areas. Service workers in hotels, restaurants, parks, stores, beaches, museums, and other attractions are all part of the industry.

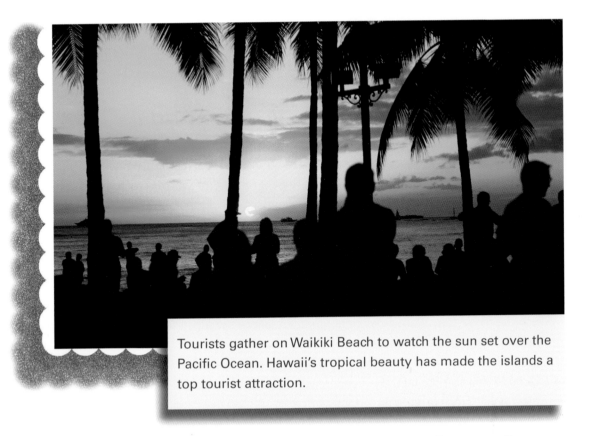

Tourists gather on Waikiki Beach to watch the sun set over the Pacific Ocean. Hawaii's tropical beauty has made the islands a top tourist attraction.

Agriculture and Related Manufacturing

Many Hawaiians earn their living from the land, making agriculture a major part of the state's economy. Hawaii's major exports include sugar, pineapples, coffee, bananas, papayas, cattle, macadamia nuts, and cut flowers. Maui leads all of the islands in sugar and pineapple production. These two crops alone make up more than 25 percent of the state's agricultural income.

Pineapple and sugarcane have long been important crops in Hawaii, and processing and shipping these crops created important manufacturing industries. Fruit canning is Hawaii's most important manufacturing industry. Other processed foods from

Working for King Sugar

By the mid-1800s, sugar production was Hawaii's number-one agricultural export. However, the plantation owners could not find enough Hawaiians to grow and harvest sugarcane. To solve this problem, they arranged for workers to come to Hawaii from Asia. These workers signed a contract stating that, in exchange for free passage to Hawaii, they would work in the sugarcane fields for three to five years. These workers were paid very little, only a few dollars a day. They were also given shelter. After their contracts were up, the workers were free to quit their jobs and find better ones. However, if workers left a plantation while they were still under contract, the police could arrest them and put them in prison. In addition, because they were foreigners, contract laborers were treated as a lower social class than white residents and native Hawaiians.

Today's sugarcane workers face very different conditions than those who came to Hawaii more than one hundred years ago. Like most other modern industries, sugar processing is now done with a lot of machines and technology. The workers in Hawaii are no longer indentured field hands. Instead, the men and women who work in the sugarcane fields and plants are highly paid, skilled workers. Although this has been good for some workers, the higher cost of labor has made sugar more expensive to produce in Hawaii. As a result, a large amount of sugar production has shifted to countries such as the Philippines and Taiwan, where labor is cheaper. Although sugar is still a major export, it can no longer be called King Sugar in Hawaii.

Workers harvest sugarcane on Oahu in the 1940s.

Hawaii include bread, candy, fruit juice, and cheese.

Military

The military is another major employer in Hawaii. More than forty thousand military personnel are stationed in the state. These workers include members from three branches of the U.S. military: the army, navy, and air force. In addition to soldiers and sailors, about fifteen thousand civilians work for the military in Hawaii as well.

A field of pineapples grows under the Hawaiian sun. Pineapples are one of Hawaii's most important crops.

Fishing

Since Hawaii is an island state, fishing is an important part of its economy. The state is a leading center for the fishing of yellowfin and bigeye tuna. Along with the commercial fishing of wild populations, Hawaii is also developing a strong aquaculture industry. This industry raises shellfish and edible seaweed on offshore farms.

Chapter 5

PEOPLE FROM HAWAII: PAST AND PRESENT

Hawaii is the birthplace or home of many famous Americans. Authors, business leaders, athletes, entertainers, and government leaders have all been residents of this island state. Here are just a few of Hawaii's famous people.

Tia Carrere (1967–) Born in Honolulu, Tia Carrere is a singer and actress who has appeared in many television shows. She has also been in movies such as *Wayne's World, Rising Sun,* and *True Lies.* Carrere voiced the role of Lilo's big sister, Nani, in the Disney animated movie and TV series *Lilo & Stitch.* She also added her voice to cartoons such as *Aloha, Scooby-Doo, American Dragon: Jake Long,* and *Duck Dodgers.*

Joseph de Veuster (1840–1889) Better known as Father Damien, Joseph de Veuster was a Belgian priest who went to Molokai in 1873 to help people with Hansen's disease. He treated them with respect and love at a time when people with the disease were feared and isolated. Father Damien died of Hansen's disease at age forty-nine. In 2009, the Catholic Church named him a saint.

James Drummond Dole (1877–1958) Born in Massachusetts, James Dole dreamed of starting a business. He moved to Hawaii in 1899 and later started a pineapple plantation and canning company. In 1922, he bought the island of Lanai and set up a 15,000-acre (6,070 hectare) pineapple plantation there. Today, his business continues as the Dole Food Company.

Hiram L. Fong (1906–2004) Hiram L. Fong was born in Honolulu and became the first American of Chinese descent elected to the U.S. Senate. He represented Hawaii from 1959 until 1976. His goal was to promote cooperation between Hawaii's ethnic groups.

Bethany Hamilton (1990–) Bethany Hamilton was born on Kauai after her parents moved to Hawaii for its fantastic surfing opportunities. When she was thirteen, Hamilton lost her left arm in a shark attack while surfing in Kauai. She returned to the water just three weeks later and went on to achieve her dream of becoming a professional surfer.

Surfer Bethany Hamilton's loss of an arm in a shark attack shocked the world. But Hamilton refused to give up her beloved sport of surfing.

Music Mix—Hawaiian Style

Music has been an important part of Hawaii's culture for centuries. Ancient Hawaiian cultures used chanting and other musical elements in their religious ceremonies. Hawaiian chants and songs also accompanied the islands' traditional dance, the hula. The Hawaiian hula originated with the Polynesian settlers. It features graceful movements of the hands, arms, and hips.

No one studied or documented Hawaiian music until after the first Europeans arrived in 1778. For the next one hundred years, Hawaiian music was influenced by European instruments, which were introduced to the islands by the new settlers. Settlers from Portugal brought with them the ukulele, a stringed instrument that has since become an important part of Hawaiian music. The Spanish brought the guitar, and Hawaiian musicians developed variations of the instrument, including the steel guitar and slack key guitar.

After the United States took control of Hawaii, Hawaiian music spread to the mainland. Between 1912 and 1930, this music grew in popularity, and those from different musical backgrounds began to incorporate Hawaiian sounds and styles into their own music. The years between 1930 and 1960 have been called the Golden Age of Hawaiian Music. During this time, Hawaiian music was adapted for orchestras and big bands. In addition, Hawaiian performers such as Lani McIntire, Sol Hoopii, and Don Ho became big stars throughout the United States.

Traditional Hawaiian music is still popular in the islands and is incorporated into other types of music. However, American popular music, such as rock, pop, and rap, has become more popular in Hawaii, influencing the music there. Several Hawaiian performers have even appeared on the popular television talent show *American Idol*! If you go to Hawaii today, you are likely to hear current popular songs on the radio, but you will also hear music that is a unique mix of traditional Hawaiian sounds and modern styles.

Don Ho (1930–2007) Don Ho was born in Honolulu and grew up in Kaneohe on Oahu. He achieved worldwide fame as a singer, comedian, and storyteller who performed hit songs such as "Tiny Bubbles." Ho was a champion of Hawaiian music and helped introduce Hawaiian culture to people around the world.

Carrie Ann Inaba (1968–) Born in Honolulu, Carrie Ann Inaba won a statewide talent contest with an original dance piece when she was just sixteen. She's had a varied career as a dancer, singer, and choreographer. Inaba has worked on different television programs and is currently a judge on the popular show *Dancing with the Stars*.

Daniel K. Inouye (1924–) Daniel K. Inouye was born in Honolulu. He served in the U.S. Army's Nisei Combat Team during World War II, where he lost his right arm in battle. He was awarded the Bronze Star, the Purple Heart, and the Congressional Medal of Honor. In 1959, he became Hawaii's first representative in Congress and the nation's first Japanese American congressman. With eight terms in the U.S. Senate, he is the third longest-serving senator in U.S. history. Inouye was on the committee that investigated Richard Nixon's involvement in the Watergate scandal.

Duke Kahanamoku (1889–1968) Duke Kahanamoku was called "the human fish" for his incredible achievements in swimming, surfing, and water polo. He won gold medals in swimming in the 1912, 1920, and 1924 Olympics. Kahanamoku also popularized the sport of surfing, delighting

Duke Kahanamoku revolutionized the sport of surfing with his daring tricks and techniques.

audiences with tricks such as riding backward and doing handstands. He is known as the father of modern surfing.

James Michener (1907–1997) Born in New York and raised in Pennsylvania, James Michener discovered the Pacific Islands while serving there during World War II. He went on to write many popular novels, including *Tales of the South Pacific*, which was made into the Broadway musical and movie *South Pacific*. Michener moved to Honolulu in 1949 and spent ten years there writing the novel *Hawaii*. He finished the book on August 21, 1959, the day Hawaii became the fiftieth U.S. state.

Bette Midler (1945–) Bette Midler was born in Honolulu and lived there until she was twenty years old. After starting her career as a singer and comedian, Midler received an Oscar nomination for her performance in the film *The Rose*. She also starred in many other movies, including *Beaches, The First Wives Club*, and *The Stepford Wives*.

Patsy Mink (1927–2002) Patsy Takemoto Mink served as a U.S. representative from Hawaii from 1965 to 1977, and again from 1990 until her death in 2002. In 1972, she helped write the historic legislation known as Title IX, which established equal rights and equal funding for women's sports in schools and communities.

Barack Obama (1961–) The nation's first African American president was born in Honolulu and lived in Hawaii for most of his childhood. After serving as a U.S. senator for Illinois, Barack Obama was elected president of the United States in 2008. He was awarded the Nobel Peace Prize in 2009.

Ellison Onizuka achieved fame as the first Hawaiian and first Asian American astronaut before his tragic death in the 1986 *Challenger* disaster.

Ellison Onizuka (1946–1986) Hawaii's first astronaut was born in Kealakekua and grew up in Hawaii. Ellison Onizuka became the first Asian American in space as part of the crew of the *Discovery* in 1985. Tragically, Onizuka died during his second space shuttle mission. He was one of the seven astronauts lost in the *Challenger* disaster in 1986.

Graham Salisbury (1944–) Graham Salisbury is a popular young adult novelist who was born and raised in Hawaii. He has set many of his award-winning novels in Hawaii, including *Under the Blood-Red Sun, Shark Bait*, and *Jungle Dogs*.

Robert Louis Stevenson (1850–1894) Born in Scotland, Robert Louis Stevenson became the hugely popular writer of adventure novels like *Treasure Island*, *Kidnapped*, and *The Strange Case of Dr. Jekyll and Mr. Hyde*. He lived in Hawaii off and on to gain health benefits from the tropical climate. His writings helped the world learn about Joseph de Veuster (Father Damien) and his work.

Golfer Michelle Wie makes a shot during the LPGA World Championships in 2005. Wie turned professional when she was just fifteen.

Michelle Wie (1989–) Michelle Wie grew up in Honolulu and began playing golf when she was just four years old. She joined the ranks of professional golfers in 2004, when she was still a teenager. That year she became the youngest person ever selected for the U.S. Curtis Cup Championship team. In 2009, Wie achieved her first victory in an LPGA event, winning the Lorena Ochoa Invitational in Mexico.

Tammy Yee (1946–) Tammy Yee is the author and illustrator of many children's books about Hawaii, including *The Tsunami Quilt* and *A Is for Aloha*. Her work reflects the stories and natural beauty of Hawaii. Yee grew up in Honolulu and worked as a nurse before becoming a writer and illustrator.

Timeline

300–1000 CE	Polynesian settlers arrive in Hawaii.
1778–1779	British explorer Captain James Cook arrives in Hawaii.
1795	Kamehameha, ruler of the island of Hawaii, conquers Oahu and three other islands.
1810	Kamehameha gains control of all the islands and becomes Hawaii's first monarch, Kamehameha I.
1819	Kamehameha II becomes king and ends the kapu system.
1820	The first Christian missionaries arrive in Hawaii.
1835	The first major sugar plantation is started on Kauai.
1840	Kamehameha III creates a new constitution that gives power to a legislature.
1891	Queen Liliuokalani comes to the throne and tries to restore power to the monarchy.
1893	Liliuokalani is overthrown by U.S. business owners and soldiers.
1894	Hawaii becomes a republic under Sanford Dole.
1898	The United States annexes Hawaii.
1900	Hawaii becomes a U.S. territory; James Dole starts his first pineapple plantation in Hawaii.
1941	Japanese bombers attack the U.S. naval base at Pearl Harbor, drawing the United States into World War II.
1959	Hawaii becomes the fiftieth U.S. state.
1993	President Bill Clinton signs a resolution apologizing for the United States' overthrow of the Hawaiian monarchy.
2002	Hawaii elects its first female governor, Linda Lingle.
2009	The Catholic Church declares Father Damien a saint.

State motto:	"The Life of the Land Is Perpetuated in Righteousness"
State capital:	Honolulu
State song:	"Hawaii Ponoi"
State flower:	Yellow hibiscus
State bird:	Nene (Hawaiian goose)
State tree:	Kukui (Candlenut)
State marine mammal:	Humpback whale
State gem:	Black coral
Statehood date and number:	August 21, 1959; fiftieth state
State nickname:	Aloha State
Total area and U.S. rank:	6,423 square miles (16,635 sq km); forty-third largest state
Population:	1,288,198
Length of coastline:	750 miles (1,207 km)

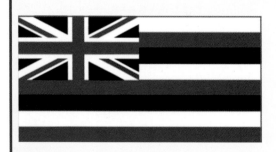

State Flag

State Seal

Highest elevation:	Mauna Kea, at 13,796 feet (4,205 m)
Lowest elevation:	Sea level at the Pacific Ocean
Major rivers:	Wailua River, Waimea River, Wailuku River, Kaukonahua Stream
Major lake:	Halalii Lake
Hottest temperature recorded:	100 degrees Fahrenheit (38 degrees Celsius) at Pahala, on April 27, 1931
Coldest temperature recorded:	12 degrees Fahrenheit (-11 degrees Celsius) at Mauna Kea, on May 17, 1979
Origin of state name:	From the native words *hawaiki* or *owyhyhee*, which mean "homeland."
Chief agricultural products:	Sugarcane, pineapples, coffee, tropical fruits, macadamia nuts, cattle, pigs, poultry
Major industries:	Tourism, agriculture, manufacturing, fishing

Nene (Hawaiian goose)

Yellow Hibiscus

GLOSSARY

agriculture The practice of farming.

annex To add or incorporate a territory.

aquaculture The farming of fish and aquatic plants under controlled conditions.

archipelago A chain or cluster of islands.

caste A system of rigid social classes set by custom, law, or religion.

constitution Basic laws that establish and run a government and that guarantee certain rights to the people.

debris The remains of something destroyed; rubble.

edible Able to be eaten.

envoy A representative of one government in its dealings with another government.

executive Having to do with the branch of government that carries out laws and runs public affairs.

federal Having to do with the national government.

feral Existing in, or having returned to, a wild state.

fertile Good for growing plants.

gorge A deep valley with steep, rocky sides.

indentured Bound by a contract to work for someone for a certain period of time.

infamy An evil reputation.

judicial Having to do with judges and courts.

legislative Having to do with making laws.

leprosy A disease that damages the nerves and skin, and can cause disfigurement.

mainland The main landmass of a country or region.

missionary A person sent to convert others to a religion and do humanitarian work.

monarchy A system of government in which one person reigns, usually a king or queen. Power is inherited, and the person rules for life.

native Having to do with people or things that originally exist in an area.

Nisei The American-born children of Japanese immigrants.

plateau An area of high, flat land.

republic A system of government in which the chief of state is not a monarch and is usually a president. Power rests with the citizens, who can vote.

territory A geographic area belonging to a government.

topography The surface features of a region.

tropical Very hot and humid.

FOR MORE INFORMATION

Department of Land and Natural Resources

Division of State Parks

P.O. Box 621

Honolulu, HI 96809

(808) 587-0300

Web site: http://www.hawaiistateparks.org

This organization provides facts about Hawaii's many state parks.

Hawaiian Historical Society

560 Kawaiahao Street

Honolulu, HI 96813

(808) 537-6271

Web site: http://www.hawaiianhistory.org

This organization gives information on many aspects of Hawaii's history.

Maui Historical Society

2375-A Main Street

Wailuku, HI 96793

(808) 244-3326

Web site: http://www.mauimuseum.org

This organization is the central hub for information on Maui's history and culture.

Web Sites

Due to the changing nature of Internet links, Rosen Publishing has developed an online list of Web sites related to the subject of this book. This site is updated regularly. Please use this link to access the list:

http://www.rosenlinks.com/uspp/hipp

FOR FURTHER READING

Dowswell, Paul. *Pearl Harbor: December 7, 1941* (Days That Shook the World). Austin, TX: Raintree Steck-Vaughn Publishers, 2003.

Goldberg, Jake, and Joyce Hart. *Hawai'i* (Celebrate the States). New York, NY: Marshall Cavendish Benchmark, 2007.

Goldsberry, U'ilani. *A Is for Aloha.* Chelsea, MI: Sleeping Bear Press, 2005.

Kent, Deborah. *Hawaii* (America the Beautiful, Third Series). New York, NY: Children's Press, 2008.

Kent, Deborah. *Hawaii's Road to Statehood* (Cornerstones of Freedom). New York, NY: Children's Press, 2004.

McAuliffe, Emily. *Hawaii Facts and Symbols* (The States and Their Symbols). New York, NY: Hilltop Books, 2000.

Middleton, Susan, and David Littschwager. *Remains of a Rainbow: Rare Plants and Animals of Hawaii.* Washington, DC: National Geographic Society, 2003.

Morrison, Susan. *Kamehameha: The Warrior King of Hawaii.* Honolulu, HI: University of Hawaii Press, 2003.

Obregón, José María. *Hawaii* (The Bilingual Library of the United States of America). New York, NY: PowerKids Press, 2005.

Quasha, Jennifer. *How to Draw Hawaii's Sights and Symbols* (Kid's Guide to Drawing America). New York, NY: PowerKids Press, 2002.

Salisbury, Graham. *House of the Red Fish.* New York, NY: Wendy Lamb Books, 2006.

Salisbury, Graham. *Under the Blood-Red Sun.* New York, NY: Delacorte Press, 1994.

Sherman, Josepha. *Queen Lydia Liliuokalani, Last Ruler of Hawaii* (On My Own Biography). Minneapolis, MN: Carolrhoda Books, 2005.

Shofner, Shawndra. *Hawaii* (This Land Called America). Mankato, MN: Creative Education, 2009.

Temple, Teri, and Bob Temple. *Welcome to Hawai'i Volcanoes National Park* (Visitor Guides). Chanhassen, MN: Child's World, 2007.

BIBLIOGRAPHY

American Academy of Achievement. "James Michener Biography." August 31, 2009. Retrieved October 18, 2009 (http://www.achievement.org/autodoc/page/mic0bio-1).

BethanyHamilton.com. "Bethany Hamilton—Soul Surfer." Retrieved October 18, 2009 (http://www.bethanyhamilton.com).

Biography.com. "Bette Midler Biography." 2009. Retrieved October 18, 2009 (http://www.biography.com/articles/Bette-Midler-9407865).

Boyle, Richard A. "Robert Louis Stevenson Biography." Retrieved October 18, 2009 (http://people.brandeis.edu/~teuber/stevensonbio.html).

Cosgrove-Mather, Bootie. "Last Days of a Leper Colony: Days, and Funerals, Dwindling for Residents of Former Leper Colony." CBSNews.com, March 22, 2003. Retrieved October 19, 2009 (http://www.cbsnews.com/stories/2003/03/22/health/main545392.shtml).

Crowe, Ellie. *Exploring Lost Hawaii: Places of Power, History, Mystery, & Magic.* Waipahu, HI: Island Heritage Publishers, 2008.

Dancing with the Stars Fan Site. "Carrie Ann Inaba Biography." September 23, 2009. Retrieved October 18, 2009 (http://www.dwts.org/page/Carrie+Ann+Inaba+Bio).

Griffiths, Zoe. "Riding the Wave Against All Odds." *National* (United Arab Emirates), October 14, 2009. Retrieved October 18, 2009 (http://thenational.ae/apps/pbcs.dll/article?AID=/20091015/SPORT/710149912/1100).

Hawaiian Volcano Observatory, U.S. Geological Survey. "Introduction to Kilauea Volcano, Hawaii." May 7, 2009. Retrieved October 5, 2009 (http://hvo.wr.usgs.gov/kilauea).

Ho Enterprises. "Don Ho Biography." Retrieved October 18, 2009 (http://www.donho.com/biography.html).

IMDb.com. "Tia Carrere Biography." Retrieved October 18, 2009 (http://www.imdb.com/name/nm0000119/bio).

JacketFlap.com. "Tammy Yee–Contact Information, Biography, Books, Blog, and Pictures." 2009. Retrieved October 18, 2009 (http://www.jacketflap.com/profile.asp?member=yeeart).

Kane, Herbert Kawainui. *Ancient Hawaii.* Captain Cook, HI: Kawainui Press, 1997.

Krainacker, Dave. "Father Damien and the Molokai Leper Colony." *Queen City News*, May 10, 2006. Retrieved October 19, 2009 (http://www.queencitynews.com/modules.php?op=modload&name=News&file=article&sid=5372).

Oahu.US. "Kahoolawe." Retrieved October 19, 2009 (http://www.oahu.us/kahoolawe.htm).

OIRC: Offshore Islet Restoration Committee. "Islets: Molokai: Huelo." Retrieved January 15, 2010 (http://www.hawaiioirc.org/OIRC-ISLETS-Molokai/OIRC-ISLETS-Molokai-Huelo.htm).

Potter, Norris W. *The Hawaiian Monarchy.* Honolulu, HI: Bess Press, 1983.

TammyYee.com. "Tammy Yee, Hawaii Children's Book Author and Illustrator." 2007. Retrieved October 18, 2009 (http://www.tammyyee.com).

Vorsino, Mary. "A Legacy of Compassion and Care: Father Damien's Remarkable Life Serves as an Inspiration to Many." *Honolulu Advertiser*, October 11, 2009. Retrieved October 12, 2009 (http://www.honoluluadvertiser.com/article/20091011/NEWS01/910110331/A + legacy + of + compassion + and + care).

INDEX

A

Apology Resolution, 22

C

Carrere, Tia, 32
Cook, James, 16–17

D

Damien, Father (Joseph de Veuster), 18,
    32, 38
Dole, James Drummond, 19, 20, 33
Dole, Sanford B., 20

F

Fong, Hiram L., 33

H

Hamilton, Bethany, 33
Hawaii
chiefs and Native Hawaiian society, 15–16,
    26
    early inhabitants of, 14–15
    and European explorers and settlers, 16–17
    islands of, 6–12
    major industries of, 28–31
    music of, 34
    plant and animal life of, 12–13
    and statehood, 5, 22
    in World War II, 20–21
Hawaii (Big Island), 6–8, 14, 15
Ho, Don, 34, 35
Honolulu, 11, 27, 32, 33, 35, 36, 37, 38
Hooper, William, 19

I

Inaba, Carrie Ann, 35
Inouye, Daniel K., 35

K

Kahanamoku, Duke, 35–36
Kahoolawe, 8, 10
Kamehameha I, 15–16, 17, 26
Kamehameha II, 17, 26
Kauai, 11, 14, 33
Kilauea, 7–8

L

Lanai, 9, 15, 19, 33
Liliuokalani, Queen, 19–20, 22

M

Maui, 8, 9, 15
Mauna Loa, 6, 7
Michener, James, 36
Midler, Bette, 36
Mink, Patsy, 36–37
Molokai, 9, 16, 18, 32

N

Niihau, 11–12

O

Oahu, 9, 11, 15, 20, 35
Obama, Barack, 37
Onizuka, Ellison, 37

S

Salisbury, Graham, 37
Stevenson, Robert Louis, 38

W

Wie, Michelle, 38

Y

Yee, Tammy, 38

About the Author

Joanne Mattern has traveled throughout the United States and loves the immense variety in the nation. Mattern enjoys history, nature, travel, and discovering new places and interesting stories. She has written more than two hundred nonfiction books for children and works in her local library. Mattern also enjoys spending time with her husband, four children, and a menagerie of pets.

Photo Credits

Cover (top left) Al Greene/Hulton Archive/Getty Images, cover (top right) © www.istockphoto.com/Robert Simon, cover (bottom) © www.istockphoto.com/Henry Price; pp. 3, 6, 14, 23, 28, 32, 39 Charles Gullung/Photonica/Getty Images; p. 4 (top) © GeoAtlas; p. 7 R. L. Christiansen, U.S. Geological Survey; p. 9 Turner & de Vries/The Image Bank/Getty Images; p. 11 Sean Rowland/ASP/Covered Images via Getty Images; pp. 13, 29 Jerry Driendl/The Image Bank/Getty Images; p. 15 The Granger Collection, New York; p. 16 Kean Collection/Hulton Archive/Getty Images; p. 21 Still Picture Records, U.S. National Archives and Records Administration; pp. 22, 24, 30 ©AP Images; p. 25 Courtesy House Majority Communications Office, Hawaii House of Representatives, 2008; p. 31 Dole Company; p. 33 Steve Robertson/ASP/Covered Images via Getty Images; p. 36 Library of Congress Prints and Photographs Division, Washington D.C.; p. 37 NASA; p. 38 Robert Laberge/Getty Images; p. 40 (left) courtesy of Robesus, Inc.; p. 41 (left) © www.istockphoto.com/Robert Fullerton; p. 41 (right) Shutterstock.com.

Designer: Les Kanturek; Editor: Andrea Sclarow; Photo Researcher: Marty Levick